No Prep. No Prop. Children's Sermons

52 Children's Sermons for Telling Children about Jesus in a Hurried World.

By Heather N. Hagler
with Ken L. Hagler

www.kenhagler.com

Credits:
Cover Design: Logan Hagler
Typing: Jillian Hagler

From the authors:
from Heather:

Our hectic pace of life has reached every part of society, including the church. Pastor and church staff are expected to do more in less time. With volunteerism down and congregational expectations on the rise, everyone involved in spreading the Gospel needs help.

No Prep No Prop Children's Sermons is a book designed for pastors, laity, and church staff facing a time crunch. Perhaps a trusted volunteer calls in sick or a schedule change leaves the children's sermon preparation to the last minute.

Everyone has experienced that last-minute panic from time to time. Imagine this typical scenario - a volunteer picks up a book of children's sermons on Saturday night to prepare for a Sunday morning message only to find all the sermons call for extensive props or rehearsals. So, they put the book aside and decide to "wing it" the next day. The results are less than the quality outreach the children need.

This book will fill the gap with Biblical, relevant, and fun children's sermons that require no props or rehearsals. These children's sermons will engage the children on their level. The wide variety of topics and Bible passages assures the reader of a message for every season.

No Prep No Prop Children's Sermons will have a place on the bookshelf of laity, clergy, and church staff. We are all looking for quality children's programming resources that can be used in the real world with real schedules.

This resource was written to meet a need I felt first hand. For three years I have served as the volunteer leader of the children's moments in my church. With a background of a Master's Degree in Christian Education, I have also served as a day camp leader, Vacation Bible School coordinator, Sunday School teacher and children's church leader. As the wife of a church planter, I have also helped others organize and plan their ministry with children in the church.

No Prep No Prop Children's Sermons will be a valuable tool to all paid and volunteer ministers reaching children.

Heather

From Ken,

To say that Heather loved children's ministry and sharing the Gospel of Jesus Christ with children is an understatement. It was her heart's passion and she was so gifted, it was a joy to watch her. Like listening to musician or admiring a painter's work, to be around Heather when she was with children was to know you were in the presence of someone called and gifted for their work.

When she set out to write this collection of children's sermons, they came from her heart and something she wanted to share to support anyone involved in children's ministry. Each has been tried out both by her and many of them by myself, too! That she passed from this earth before getting it published was not easy for her to accept. I wish I knew then what I know now but am so thankful her dream and hope and gifts can go on.

Words cannot express what this project means to me. Getting this book to publication has been a work of love and full of memories. I am so thankful for the input I got from so many friends and people who loved Heather. It has also been a work of our family, both of Heather's children are part of this work. Logan, our son, designed the cover and Jillian, our daughter, retyped the original manuscript for this publication (the digital copy had been lost and after Heather's death, in going through her notes, I found the original manuscript).

Special thanks go out to Jane Lathem, DeDe Reilly, Brent Van Hook, Connie Cash, and Chandler Bolt and the folks at Self-Publishing School for your continued wisdom and guidance.

May Heather's words and ministry bless you,
Ken

Table of Contents

Old Testament

New Testament

For Special Days

Old Testament

1. Creation Caretakers...Genesis 1:27-28

Once there was a famous carpenter who was known all over the world for making beautiful furniture. He used the strongest and most sturdy wood and the best tools.

Two families were good friends of the carpenter. One day the carpenter made two tables - one for each family. He used strong wood. He took great care measuring each piece, so they fit together exactly. He even carved detailed designs in the wood. Each table was not only strong and well-made, but also beautiful.

The carpenter gave each family their table. He told them, "These tables are some of my best work. I am very proud of them. I am giving them to you because I want you to be happy. I took time, energy, and love to make them. By using them you will show me how much you love me. Use these tables every day and remember me."

Each family was very pleased to have such a beautiful table. They used them every day. The first family ate all their meals sitting at the strong table. They sometimes spilled milk or food on the table, but they always cleaned up. Once a week they polished the wood until it shone.

The second family also ate all their meals at the beautiful table in their kitchen. They also sometimes spilled milk or food on the table. But they did not clean the table very well. They did not polish it. The children put their feet on the table. The adults were careless and banged their chairs into the table. This table soon became dirty and dull. It had scratches on the top and dents in the legs.

During a visit to the first family's house, the carpenter was asked to sit down for a meal at the clean, polished table. He was happy to see the piece of furniture he had worked so hard to build was used and cherished.

The next week, the carpenter went to the second family's house. When he saw their table, he was very disappointed. The top of the table he had taken so long to sand, and polish was all scratched. The designs he had carved into the legs were spoiled by the dents and dirt.

He said, "I am so disappointed. When I see how you have treated my table, the gift I made because I loved you, I know you don't have any respect for me. If you don't take care of my creation, I know you don't love me."

(Read Genesis 1:27-28.) God made the world and everything in it, just like the carpenter made the table in our story. God gave the world to people, just like the carpenter gave his gift to the families. How have you or someone you know taken care of God's creation? (Allow for responses.)

How have you seen people hurting the earth and not taking care of it? What are some ways you can take care of the earth? Give time for answers.

Let's remember that the earth is God's creation and a gift to us. He has asked us to take care of it.

Prayer: God, thank you for the world and everything in it. Please help us to be wise in caring for this wonderful gift. Amen.

2. Building Altars...Genesis 12:8, Exodus 17:15, Joshua 4:9

Raise your hand if you have ever built something. Tell me one thing that you have built. (Give time for the children to share their experiences.)

In the Bible we read many stories where people are building. Noah built the ark. The Israelites built a special tent where they could worship God on their wilderness journey. Solomon worked with others to build the temple in Jerusalem.

Many Bible stories tell us about God's people building altars. An altar is a special place to worship God or to remember God's goodness. In today's world we use wood or metal to make altars. In the earliest Bible stories altars were made by piling rocks on top of each other.

I'm going to tell you about some altars in the Bible. Listen carefully. When you hear about someone building an altar, you can use your hands to pretend to build your own altar. (Demonstrate the hand motions by gently tapping your fists, one on top of the other.)

Abraham was a man who lived long ago. God called Abraham to leave the place where he lived and travel to the land that God would give him and his family. Many times, when Abraham traveled he built an altar (make hand motions) to help him and his family remember that God was with them.

Moses was a great leader of God's people. With God's power Moses helped the Israelites travel to the land God promised them. On their journey, they fought with the army of another people called the Amalekites. The Israelites won the battle. Moses built an altar (make hand motions) to help the Israelites remember that God had given them victory over their enemies.

Joshua was also a great leader. To reach the promised land, the Israelites had to cross the Jordan River. God's power dried up the river and Joshua led the people across. After they had crossed the river, Joshua told some of the people to take rocks from the dry riverbed to make an altar (make hand motions) this altar would help them remember how God had stopped the water from the Jordan river, so the Israelites could cross.

All these altars were built to help God's people remember how God had been with them and helped them. Tell me about a time in your life when God has been with you and helped you. (Allow for responses.) Maybe you could build an altar (make hand motions) to remember that time.

The altar doesn't have to be made of rocks in your yard. You could have special box for a collection of items to remember God's care for you. Maybe you can draw a picture of your baseball game to remember that God helped you to play your best. You can find a leaf from a camping trip you took with your family to remember God's beautiful creation. You could even put in a piece of clean dental floss to remember how God helped you to be brave at the dentist office. Anything at all can help you build your altar (make hand motions) to remember God's love, protection, and gifts for you.

Prayer: God, thank you for taking care of us. Please help us to remember your love and protection every day. Help us to find ways to build altars to remember. Amen.

3. Family Troubles...Genesis 25:19-34

Let me tell you about two brothers – Jake and Eddie. Jake and Eddie were in the same family, but they were very different. They didn't look alike. They liked to do different things. After school, Jake loved more than anything to be at home, playing computer games and helping his mom around the house. Eddie liked to be outside, riding his bike.

From the time they were born, Jake and Eddie were fighting. Do you fight with your brothers or sisters? Jake and Eddie fought over everything: who got the biggest serving of dessert after dinner, who got to pick the movie they watched on television, who brushed their teeth first at night.

Eddie was the older brother, and he had more privileges. For his birthday, Eddie's parents brought him a new bicycle. Eddie loved that bicycle. Because he was older he was able to go farther from home and be out later in the evening.

Jake wanted a new bicycle, too, but his parents said he was too young. So, Eddie and Jake fought about the new bicycle.

One day, Eddie had been out riding his new bike all over the neighborhood. When he came home he was hungry and tired. Eddie walked into the kitchen and found Jake. Jake had just finished helping his mom make a huge pan of brownies. They were cooled and ready to be eaten. Eddie was so hungry; he wanted a big brownie.

He asked Jake to get him a brownie. But Jake refused. He said, "I was the one who helped mom make them, so they are mine. Make your own brownies."

"Oh, Jake!" Eddie said, "I don't know how to make brownies. You're always the one who is helping mom around the house. You know how to cook and I don't. Just give me one brownie. I'm about to starve to death."

Jake saw his chance to take advantage of the situation. He thought of a plan to get what he wanted- Eddie's new bike. SO, Jake said, "Ok, Eddie, I'll give you a brownie - if you trade me your new bike for it."

Eddie was so hungry he didn't even care. He said, "Fine, fine - take the dumb bike. Just give me a brownie!"

When Jake and Eddie traded the brownie for the bike, they both made bad choices. Eddie didn't value his bike and traded it for a brownie. Jake didn't want to help his brother; he only wanted to help himself.

Do you have any problems with your brothers and sisters? Do you ever make bad choices when it comes to your brothers and sisters? How do you think God wants you to treat your family? (Give time for the children to answer.)

Eddie soon realized that he made a mistake in trading his bike for a brownie. He was very angry with Jake. But after a while, Eddie and Jake realized that they both were acting in a way that was making God and their parents very sad. They decided to stop fighting and work on getting along.

God can give Jake and Eddie the strength and wisdom to get along with each other. He can do the same for you if you struggle in getting along with your family.

Prayer: God, thank you for families. Please help us to live together and love each other. Amen.

4. Thank you, God, For Feelings...Psalm 35:1-3, Psalm 42:11, Psalm 118:6, Psalm 147:1

Do you like to make silly faces? Show me your silliest face. (Allow children to respond.) Can you make faces that show feelings? (Give time for children to make each face.) Can your face show feeling scared? Angry? Sad? Happy?

God has given us all wonderful faces to show our feelings. Sometimes we call "feelings" our "emotions". I'm going to tell some stories about emotions. When I finish telling the story, make a face that shows the feelings that go along with the story. Give the children time to respond following each story.

The first story is about a girl named Julia. One-night Julia was sleeping when the sounds of a thunderstorm woke her. She saw lightning outside her window. She heard thunder. Then, the lights went out in her house. Can you make a face to show me how Julia felt?

In our second story, a boy named Michael loved to play soccer. He practiced with his team every week, and he was very excited about their first game. When the day of the game came, Michael heard raindrops on his bedroom window. Soon after, his coach called and said that the game was canceled because of rain. Show me in your face how you think Michael feels.

Listen to our third story about a girl named Savannah. Savannah loved to paint pictures. She worked very hard to make her pictures beautiful. Whenever she painted Savannah kept a small cup of water close by to clean her paintbrush. One day while she was painting a picture, her little sister, who was watching, accidentally knocked over the cup of water and spilled it all over Savannah's painting. Make a face to show how Savannah might feel.

Our last story is about a boy named Ethan. Ethan's family had a special celebration for him on his birthday. His family took Ethan to his favorite restaurant for dinner. After dinner they ate cake and ice cream, and Ethan opened his presents. Can you make a face to show me how Ethan felt?

Listening to these stories brought up all kinds of emotions. Why do you think God gave us emotions? (Allow for responses.) When we are scared, it's a warning that there may be danger. We may need to get help to be safe. When we feel sad or mad we know something around us is not right and needs to be changed. Glad feelings are God's gift to bring us happiness. All our emotions are useful. They are all given by God for a reason. We should not ignore them. When we have strong emotions like anger, fear, or sadness, we can talk to an adult we trust and talk to God. When we are happy, we can share that feeling with everyone around! Let's thank God for our feelings.

Prayer: God, thank you for feelings. Please help us to pay attention to our feelings and what they are trying to tell us. Please help us to find adults and others to share our feelings. Amen.

5. The Smartest Person In The World...Psalm 139:1-4, Psalm 147:5

Who do you think is the smartest person in the world? (Allow for the children to answer.) Is God as smart as (add a name the children mentioned)? Does God know how many stars are in the sky? How many stars do you think there are in the sky? Does God know how many fish are in the ocean?

Let's think about people. How many people are alive in the world today? Do you think God knows the answer to that question? I think we can safely say that God knows everything. The Bible tells us that God even knows how many hairs are on your head! (Try to count the hairs on one of the children's heads.) God's knowledge about the world and about us is amazing.

Do you know what else is amazing? God knows all about us and still loves us! He not only knows all the good things, but He knows the bad things too. He knows when we are angry, when we do something we shouldn't do, and when we are afraid. He knows everything about us and he still loves us and cares about us. There is nothing we will ever do that would make God stop loving us. God knows all about us and loves us anyway.

Prayer: God, thank you that you don't stop loving us when we do something that makes you sad. Help us to hold on to that wonderful love and show that love to others. Amen.

6. Guard Your Heart...Proverbs 4:23

What does the word "guard" mean to you? (Allow for answers.) A guard can be someone who watches over something. A guard keeps safe something that is valuable. A guard at a bank makes sure bad guys don't steal money at night.

The Bible tells us that we have something special to guard. (Read Proverbs 4:23.) What do you think that means? Should we stand watch over our own bodies and the hearts in our chests? (Allow for responses.) The heart in your body is very valuable. Without your heart your body couldn't live.

This passage means something more. When the Bible talks about your heart it means the parts of your personality that makes you who you are - what you think about, everything you like or don't like, all your fears, and everything that makes you happy. When you think about it that way, you can better understand how valuable the heart can be.

When the Bible says to 'guard your heart,' it means you should be very careful what goes into your heart. How does something get into your heart? Your heart is filled in many ways- the television shows you watch, the friends you spend time with, the books you read, the games you play- and many other ways, too. All these ideas, words and thoughts go into your mind and heart to make you who you are.

Why should you guard all these things that go into you? If you allow things inside you that aren't good, like television shows or music with bad words or movies with a lot of fighting or rude behavior, those bad words and behaviors become a part of you. When you get angry or upset all the bad inside you comes out.

I know you don't want to be full of those things because they make God sad. We want our hearts to be full of kind words, friendships, respect, and trust. We should be brave guards of our hearts to only let in good ideas, words, pictures, and thoughts.

Prayer: Jesus, please help us to be brave guards of our hearts. Please help us to be wise in choosing what goes into our hearts. Thank you for all the wisdom and teaching that come to us in the Bible. Amen.

7. Friend Puzzle...Proverbs 17:17

(Today the children will be creating a living puzzle on the floor of the children's moments area. If you have a small group of children, ask some adults to join your group and complete the puzzle.)

(As the children work together you may have some ask about body parts that aren't included in the puzzle, such as the nose or stomach. You can say, "A friend is made of other parts, too. Today we don't have time to talk about every part. This is only a small list to help us think about what makes a good friend.)

Raise your hand and each of you can take turns telling me the name of one of your friends. (Allow for responses.)

We're going to put together a puzzle that will help us think about what makes a good friend. You are all going to be the pieces. We'll put the friend puzzle together on the floor.

Have the children clear a place on the floor in front of their group that everyone can see. As you read each part and its description, call up a child or children to lie on the floor to create the puzzle.

First, we need the brain. (Have a child curl up in a ball on the floor to be the brain.) The brain of a good friend will help you think of solutions to problems and will help you think o ways to have fun.

On either side of the brain we have ears. (On either side of the "brain" have two children lie in semi circles to look like ears.) A good friend's ears will listen to a joke or to your worries.

On the head we also have eyes. (Under the "brain" have two children curl up in balls to be the eyes.) The eyes of a good friend will help to see if trouble is coming. They'll also see your best new shoes.

Next, we have a mouth. (Select a child to lie under the eyes in a semi-circle to be a mouth.) A good friend's mouth will never tell our secrets.

Another piece of a good friend is the heart. (Have another child lie under the mouth curled up in a ball to be the heart.) The heart of a good friend will trust you.

(Select two children to be arms. Have them lie straight on the floor diagonally from the heart.) Another piece of a good friend is the arms. A good friend's arms can help pull you along when you're climbing up a steep hill.

The legs are another part of a good friend. (Have two children lie straight, perpendicular to the "heart" to be the legs.) A good friend's legs will stand tall when they stand up for you if someone picks on you.

The last part of a good friend we'll talk about today are the feet. (Have two children curl in a ball under each leg to be feet.) The feet of a good friend will be ready to run and play with you.

Once all the children are situated say, "Wow! We've made our good friend." We have talked about what makes a good friend. When you're playing with your friends or making a new friend, let's remember what we have learned. Let's all be good friends to each other.

Have the children sit up where they are in the puzzle for the prayer.

Prayer: God, thank you for good friends. Please help us, as we go through the week to be a good friend to those we meet. Amen.

8. Friends In Common...Proverbs 22:24-25

What do you like to do for fun? Do you do any of these things with your friends? What do your friends like to do for fun? Do you like the same things? (Give some time for the children to answer the questions.)

What makes you laugh? Do you and your friends laugh at the same things? What makes you angry? Do you and your friends get angry at the same things? (Allow for responses.) (Make sure everyone who wants to talk gets a chance. But be firm and allow time for all the point of the talk. Often children are so excited to share their stories they can fill the entire time you have together!)

I'm sure you and your friends like many of the same things. That's why you are friends! When you like the same things as another person, we say you "have a lot in common."

Have you ever found that once you became friends with someone, you started acting like that person- or they started acting like you? Maybe not all the time or always, but you and your friends have more in common when you spend a lot of time together. Sometimes it's fun to have a lot in common with someone, to share games you like to play or movies you like to watch.

But what if your friend has a bad habit? Maybe they say words you aren't allowed to say. If you spend a lot of time with them, you may start to say those bad words too.

(Read Proverbs 22:24-25.) The Bible tells us to be careful when we pick our friends because we will take on the habits of the people we spend time with. When we choose our friends, we need to watch both their good and bad behavior. If someone has a lot of problems with the way they act- if they have a bad temper or they don't take care of their toys- we should think hard about being a close friend of theirs.

We should look for friends with whom we have good in common. Then our good behavior will grow together as we become better friends.

Prayer: God, thank you for friends. Thank you for the Bible that teaches us about making good friends. Please help us to be wise when we are choosing friends. Please guide us to the people who will be our good friends. Help us to be a good friend. Amen.

9. Difficult Choices...Daniel 6:1-23

Every day Gods asks us to do things to help him build his kingdom on earth. I am going to read off a list of things you might choose to do in a day. If you think doing these things would make God happy, put up your hand. If you think these things would be easy, wave your hand while its up.

(Read off each activity, pausing to allow the children to raise their hands. After reading each activity, ask the children if doing these activities is easy or hard, and allow time for them to wave their hands or keep them still.) Here is a list of activities to include: praying, reading the Bible, throwing paper airplanes in Sunday school, standing up for someone who is being bullied, saying an unkind word to someone who is mean to you, inviting a friend to Sunday school.

Some of the activities I read would not make God happy, like using unkind words. Some of them would make God happy, like praying or standing up for someone in trouble. Some of the actions that make God happy are easy to do, and some are hard. What makes some hard to do? Some responses include: I don't know what to say, I don't want to make friends angry, or I am afraid.

In our Bible we read a story of a man named Daniel. He knew that God wanted him to pray, but he also knew that when he did pray, he would get in trouble with the people who ruled the place where he lived. For Daniel, doing something that would make God happy was very hard. But God gave him the courage, and God protected Daniel when he did the right thing.

The Bible tells that God will always help us to do what is right. We might be afraid, and it may not be easy, but we know that God is with us.

Prayer: God, thank you for helping us to follow you. Please make us brave and strong to do the things that make you happy. Amen.

New Testament

10. Commercials...Matthew 10:7

How many of you watch television? Do you like the commercials? If I were to make up a commercial for our church, what should I say? (Allow the children to respond.) A commercial will show the good parts of a product and tries to get the person to buy that product.

Did you know you can be a commercial for Jesus? If others around you know that you are a Christian, they will be watching you to see if you act in a way that shows you love Jesus. When we speak kindly to each other and when we treat others as we want to be treated, we show those who are watching how wonderful life is when you love Jesus. They will see that we are not afraid, because we know God is with us. They will see that we are able to do the right thing even when it's hard because we have God's help. They will see that living a life loving Jesus is wonderful! And they may want to become Christians too.

Just like a commercial for Jesus, we can show how great life is when we live in a way that makes Jesus happy. And those who watch our lives may want to try Jesus for themselves. Remember how you live can be a commercial for living life for Jesus!

Prayer: Jesus, please help us to live in a way that is pleasing to you. Please help us to show your wonderful way of living to the world around us. Amen.

11. That's Impossible!...Matthew 14:22-33

How many of you have ever been on a boat? Have you ever been on a boat in a storm? How did it feel? (After each question, allow for responses.)

In the Bible we read about a time Jesus' disciples were in a boat on a lake during a storm. The storm came at night. The wind was blowing so strong that the water from the lake was going in the boat.

Jesus wasn't in the boat. He was on land, up on the hillside, praying. In the middle of the night, in the middle of the storm the disciples saw Jesus. They didn't know it was him at first because he was coming out to meet them in the boat. He was coming out to them by walking on the water!

When the disciples first saw him, they thought he was a ghost. When they realized it was Jesus, Peter said, "Jesus, if it is really you, tell me to come out so I can walk on the water, too."

Jesus told Peter, "Come on!"

Peter stepped out of the boat and began to walk on the water just like Jesus. But then Peter looked around at the wind and the waves, he was afraid. He started to sink. He called out for help, and Jesus reached out, grabbed him, and pulled him up. Then the wind and the waves were quiet.

What an amazing story! This is an amazing and true story. Everything about this story really happened. Walking on water seems impossible. But with Jesus's help, Peter was able to do it.

How would you have felt if you were Peter and you saw Jesus walking on the water in a storm? Would you have tried to walk on the water, even though it seems that it can't be done? (Give each child a chance to answer.)

Even today Jesus wants us to do things that seem impossible. When Jesus first asks us to do something we may think, "Jesus, that's impossible!"

I'm not saying that we should go to the nearest swimming pool and try to walk on the water, but Jesus will give us the strength to do things we think are impossible. When your brother or sister or friend says something mean to you, is it impossible for you to hold your temper and not say anything rude back to them? Even if you think you can't do it, Jesus will give you the strength to watch your words. When your friends dare you to do something you know is against the rules at school, is it impossible to stand up to the crowd and don't do it? Even if you think you can't do it, Jesus will give you the courage to do what is right.

Jesus loves you. If you ask for his help you can do amazing things!

Prayer: Jesus, please help us when we want to follow you. Please help us to be brave and to trust you when you ask us to do some thing we think is impossible. Thank you for giving us the strength to do what you ask of us. Amen.

11/15/20

12. Keys...Matthew 16:13-20

Today let's talk about keys. What is a key? Why do we use keys? (Give time for the children to answer.) Keys help us get in a door or open a lock. We usually lock up something when it is very valuable and important.

One day when Jesus was talking with the disciples, he told Peter that he would give Peter the key to heaven. What do you think he meant by that? Do you think heaven has a big door with a lock on it to keep people out?

When we have a key, we have a special way to get into a place that is very important. I think Jesus was talking about how important heaven is. I think he was talking about a special way we can get into heaven. Do you know how we can get to heaven? (Allow for responses.)

The way to get into heaven is to believe that Jesus is God's son, and that he died on the cross and came back to life. If we believe that, we will go to heaven when we die. That is the key to heaven!

When Jesus taught his disciples, Jesus gave them the key to heaven. When he died on the cross, Jesus gave all who believed in him the key to heaven.

Sometimes we use keys to lock something away that is very special because we want to keep it hidden or secret. But heaven is one thing we shouldn't keep secret. Jesus told us we should share the key to heaven with everyone. We should tell everyone the special way to get into heaven- to believe in Jesus!

Prayer: Jesus, thank you for opening the door of heaven to us. Please help us as we share this wonderful key with others. Amen.

13. The Unforgiving Servant...Matthew 18:21-35

Today we are going to talk about a big word – forgiveness. What does it mean when you forgive someone? (Allow for answers.) What does it mean when God forgives us? When we forgive, we may remember what happened that hurt us, but we make the choice not to hold that wrong in our minds or count it against the person who hurt us.

In the Bible we read many stories Jesus told to help us love in a way that pleases God. One-day Jesus told a story about forgiveness. In the story there was a king who has a servant who owed him lots of money – maybe a million dollars. He called the servant in and told him to pay back the money he owed him. The servant didn't have the money. He asked the king for patience; he said he would pay the king back the money. The king was a good man and he knew the servant couldn't repay him, so he told the servant, "I forgive you. You don't have to pay the money you owe me."

Later that day the same servant went out and met one of his friends who owed him a smaller amount of money – maybe ten dollars. The servant was so angry with the friend who owed him ten dollars that he grabbed him by the collar and said, "Pay me what you owe me right now!" The friend didn't have any money. He said, "Please forgive me! I can't pay you right now!"

But the servant wouldn't forgive him. He had his friend put in jail until he could pay back what he owed.

When the king heard about this, he was so angry. He called the servant in and told him, "I forgave you when you couldn't pay me the money you owed me. You should have forgiven your friend in the same way that I forgave you." Then the king had the servant thrown in jail until he could pay back the money he owed to the king.

Why would Jesus tell this story? He wanted us to remember how important it is to forgive each other. The servant had been shown forgiveness by the king, but then he turned around and didn't forgive his friend.

God forgives us when we do things that are wrong. He doesn't hold it against us or stop loving us. We should do the same for each other. Because God forgives us, we should forgive each other.

Prayer: God, thank you for forgiveness. Please help us to forgive others in the same way that you forgive us. Amen.

14. The Obedient Son...Matthew 21:28-31

Jesus told many stories to help us understand God and the way to live to make God happy. One story is about a dad who had two sons. One day the dad asked his sons to clean their rooms. One of the sons said, "Okay, Dad- I'll do it!" but then he started reading a new comic book, and then he found his new soccer ball and remembered that he must practice, and then he was tired and wanted to watch television. He never cleaned his room.

When the dad asked his other son to clean his room, he said "No way!" Later he was sad that he disobeyed his dad, and he cleaned his room.

Which of the sons did what his dad asked him to do? (Allow for answers.)

Let's think about what that story means to us. Suppose we hear in Sunday school that God wants us to be kind to our brothers and sisters and friends. When you hear God's teaching that we should be kind to others, it's like God is asking us, "Will you be kind to others today?" What do you say when God asks you that?

Suppose you went home after church and your brother or sister or friend borrows your bike without asking. What would you do? What would God want you to do? Would you do what you promised when God asked you in Sunday school to be kind to others? Or will we be like the son in the story who promised to do something that his dad asked, and then didn't do it? Give the children time to answer each question.

If we don't back up our words with actions, our words don't mean much. If we say to God, "Yes, I will do what you ask me to do," and then don't do it, our promises are useless. God wants us to follow through with our promises.

Prayer: God, thank you for speaking to us in the Bible. Please help us to hear you, and obey you. Please give us the strength to keep our promises we make to you. Amen.

15. Tell The World!...Matthew 28:16-20

(After asking each question allow for responses.)

How many of you ate breakfast this morning? What did you have to eat? Did you feed yourself? Who taught you to feed yourself? Why is it important to eat and feed yourself?

How many of you can read? Who taught you to read? Why is it important to know how to read? (Reassure those who cannot read yet that they will learn soon).

How many of you love Jesus? Who teaches you about Jesus? Why is it important to know about Jesus? To know you are loved no matter what you do, to know he is always with you and will help you when you are afraid or tempted to do something wrong, to know you will go to heaven to live with Jesus when you die.

Since there are so many wonderful things about knowing and loving Jesus, those who tell other people about Jesus have a very important job to do. The last instruction that Jesus gave to his disciples before Jesus went back to heaven was to go and tell everyone about him. Jesus told them to tell everyone, not only in Jerusalem where they were, but all nations.

The command was not only for the disciples - it's for us today, too. Jesus told us we should tell the whole world about Him. That's a lot of people! Let's start with those people we see every day- how can we tell our friends about Jesus? What about the people we see at school? What about the people who live in our neighborhood? Who are some other people we can talk to about Jesus? (Give each child a time to share their answers.)

Sometimes it can be scary to tell others about Jesus, or it may seem like too big of a job for us, but Jesus promises to always be with us and to help us tell others about him. We know Jesus always keeps his promises. He will always help us as we follow his teaching and obey him.

Prayer: Jesus, we are so glad that you keep your promises. Thank you for your promise to be with us as we tell others about you. Please help us to be brave and give us the words to say as we tell the world about you. Amen.

11/1/20

16. Jesus the, Super Hero…Mark 4:35-39

Raise your hand if you know about superheroes. Call out the name of your favorite superhero. (Give the children time to respond.) Let's play a game called, "Guess the superhero. I'm going to say some facts about a superhero. Raise your hand when you think you know which superhero I am describing. After reading the characteristics of a superhero, pause and choose one child with their hand raised to give the answer.

The first superhero can fly though the air. He is very strong. His costume has a big "s" on the front of his suit. (Superman)

The second superhero has a blue and red costume. His super powers come from a bug. He spins webs and uses webs to fly. (Spiderman)

The next super hero drives a special black car with tools for catching bad guys. His headquarters are in a cave. His symbol is a black bat. (Batman)

The last super hero doesn't wear a special costume. He has the power to make sick people well and blind people see. He even brought dead people back to life. He had powers over wind, water, and storms. If you ask him to come into your heart, he will be with you forever. (Jesus)

Have you ever thought about Jesus as a superhero? One of the jobs of a superhero is saving people in trouble. Let's listen to a story about a time when Jesus' friends were in trouble and he saved them. (Read Mark 4:35-39)

Does that sound like a superhero? Jesus is like a superhero, and much more. Jesus is God's son. When we ask Jesus into our hearts, He will be our superhero. He helps us to be brave when we are scared. He gives us wisdom when we make hard choices for God. Jesus is the most super of all the superheroes.

Prayer: Jesus, thank you for coming to earth. Thank you for showing your power to the disciples. Thank you for showing your power to us. Please help us to trust you with all our hearts and lives. Please give us your power to make good choices and live for you. Amen.

17. Rules...Mark 12:28-34

What rules do you have at home? (Some children may answer: clean up my room, pick up my toys, use good manners while eating, keep your hands to yourself.)

Which do you think is the most important rule? Why? (Give the children a chance to share their ideas.)

Let's think about some of the rules God has given us. Can you name any? Don't lie or cheat, remember the sabbath, honor your parents.

Once a teacher asked Jesus, "Which of God's rules is the most important?" What do you think he said? He told them, "The most important rule is: love God with all your heart, mind, strength and soul. The second most important rule is: love other people in the same way that you love yourself."

Why do you think Jesus picked these rules? (Allow for responses.) Jesus picked these rules because when you follow these rules it's much easier to follow the others. What if someone said, "I love God, but I don't want to pray or read my Bible or go to church."? Would you believe that they really love God? When you love God, then you want to follow His other rules about reading the Bible, praying, and going to church,

What if someone said, "I love others,' but then said rude things to their parents and always wanted to be first in every game they played with their friends? When we love others the same way we love ourselves it is easier to use kind words and put others first.

Jesus knew that if we keep the two most important rules- love God and love others then following the other rules of the Bible would be much easier.

Prayer: thank you for teaching us. Please make us strong to love God and love others. Please help us to live in way that makes you happy. Amen.

18. Old John...Luke 3:1-6

Once there was a man named John. He lived in the mountains in an old cabin, far from other people. He wore old clothes. He ate berries and plants that grew in the forest and the animals that he hunted. He used the animal skins for clothes. Old John had long hair and a beard - in the woods there aren't too many places to get a haircut! All day, Old John traveled around the woods, telling everyone he met about Jesus: campers, hikers, forest rangers, workers in the campground gift shops, everyone. Old John became well known around the area.

How would you feel if you and your family were out on a camping trip and Old John came up and started telling you about Jesus? Do you think God can use someone like Old John to tell other people about Jesus? (Allow for children to respond)

Old John isn't a real person; he's just a story. But there was a real man who lived a long time ago. This man lived out in the wilderness, he ate bugs and wild honey. He wore animal skins for clothes. And he told everyone about the Savior who was coming - Jesus. Do you know the name of that person? John the Baptist.

John the Baptist lived during the time of Jesus, and we can read about John in our Bibles. His job was to get the people of Israel ready for Jesus and his message.

If you lived in the Bible times, would you have gone into the wilderness to hear John the Baptist? Do you think that God can use someone like John the Baptist? (Allow for responses.)

The Bible tells us God did use John the Baptist in many ways. He baptized Jesus in the Jordan River. He taught the people that God's kingdom was coming. John the Baptist reminded the people of the things they had done to make God sad. He told them that they could return to God and tell God that they were sorry for the wrong that they had done.

Do you think that God can use someone who wears old clothes to do his work? Do you think God can use someone with long hair? Can God use someone who is very old or someone who is very young?

God can use anyone. When you feel that God wants to use you to tell others about Jesus, be brave! Don't think that just because you are young, or you don't have the right clothes, or don't go to the right school, you can't tell others about Jesus. Be brave! God will help you. Remember John the Baptist.

Prayer: God, thank you for loving me. Please help us to listen to you when you talk with us, when you ask us to tell others about you, please help us to be brave. Please help us to tell others about you and your love. Amen.

19. Let's Have a Party!...Luke 14:15-24

Have you ever been to a party? What kind of party was it? What did you do there? (Allow the children to answer after each question.)

Let's pretend we're going to have a party at our church. Tell me one thing we need to do to get ready for the party. (Food, games, decorations, invitations.)

What is the most important part of a party? I think the most important part of a party is the guests. We couldn't have a party if no one came. Our party wouldn't be much fun if we had no guests.

Jesus told a story about a party. Once there was a man who planned a wonderful party. When everything was ready, he sent his servants to bring in the guests. But the people who were invited wouldn't come. They had all kinds of reasons, and they sent messages saying that they couldn't come to the party.

What was the man going to do? He had everything ready-the food was made, and the house was cleaned. But he couldn't have a party without guests. So he told his servants to go out in the streets and gather up everyone they could find. The people out on the streets would be the guests at the party.

What do you think Jesus was trying to teach us when he told that story? (Allow for answers.) In this story God is the man who has planned the celebration. God has made a beautiful place in heaven for everyone who is in his family. God has prepared everything we need in heaven.

Then God invited everyone to be a part of his family and join the party in heaven when we die. But some people turn away the invitation. Some people don't want to ask God into their heart. They don't want to be a part of God's family. These people say "no" to the invitation to the wonderful party.

How sad! Do you ever want to be part of the party God has planned? How can we say "Yes" to God's invitation? Let Jesus come into your heart. Allow Jesus to be King of your life. When we love Jesus with all our hearts and become part of God's family, then we are a part of the party! Let's celebrate!

Prayer: God, thank you for preparing a party for us. Please help us to say "yes" to your invitation. Help us to enjoy being a part of your family every day. Amen.

20. Sunny Days...Luke 24:13-35

Do you like sunny days? Or do you like to watch a storm? During a storm where does the sun go? (Allow for responses.) During the day, the sun is always there in the sky, but during a storm the sun is behind clouds, so we can't see it. The sun is still there, we just don't recognize it because of the clouds.

We've learned from reading the Bible that God is always with us. But sometimes we may feel that God is far away, just like when the sun goes behind a cloud during a storm. When we are sad or something bad happens, we wonder if God cared or if God is with us. Just like we may wonder if the sun is still in the sky during a storm.

There is a story in the Bible about the followers of Jesus who were very sad and thought God was far away. After Jesus died on the cross, his followers were very sad. Two of Jesus' followers were walking one day, talking about everything that had happened to Jesus. They had heard some disciples say Jesus had risen from the dead, but many hadn't seen him yet.

As they walked, they came upon another person walking on the same road. The two followers of Jesus began to tell the man about Jesus and all that had happened to him. The man was Jesus, but they didn't recognize him! He began to talk with them and teach them, but they didn't know it was Jesus.

After walking for a while, they stopped to eat. When they sat down together, they recognized him- it was Jesus! Jesus had been with them all along, teaching them, and they didn't recognize him.

The followers were sad and discouraged because they thought Jesus was dead, but he was alive and with them, teaching them. When they realized he was with them they were happy and amazed.

Are you going through a hard time right now? Maybe you are sad, afraid, or discouraged and feel like God isn't with you. Remember, God is always with us, even though we may not recognize him. Like the sun is shining during the day, even though the storm may hide it, Jesus is always with us.

Prayer: Jesus, thank you that you are always with us, even during hard times. Thank you that you are teaching and walking with us when we are afraid or sad. Please help us to recognize you. Amen.

21. Mud Pies!...John 9:1-7

Have you ever played in the dirt? Do you like to make mud pies? (Let the children share their experiences.)

Did you know Jesus made mud pies? We can read in the Bible about a time when Jesus met a man who was blind. Jesus wanted to help the man to see. Jesus took some dirt in his hand and spit into the dirt. That made the dirt wet and muddy. Then Jesus took the mud and put it on the man's eyes. Jesus told the man to go wash his eyes, and when he did, he could see again! It was a miracle!

Jesus used some ordinary dirt to cause something wonderful to happen; he healed a blind man's eyes. Jesus used something very ordinary - the dirt - to show God's love and do something amazing.

Do you ever have days when you feel just ordinary? I know I do. I'm always surprised when I see God's love in my life because I'm really no one special. But in God's eyes we are all special and can be used by him to do wonderful things. Do you ever think, "I'm just a kid, there's not much I can do to show others God's love?" We've learned from our story today that's not true! God shows his love through ordinary things and ordinary people every day.

Prayer: Jesus, thank you for coming to earth. Thank you for using ordinary things to do your work. Please use us to reach out to others. Amen.

22. The Shepherd's Voice...John 10:1-5

In the Bible Jesus told stories about sheep. What do you know about sheep? (Answers include: they live in groups called flocks, a shepherd takes care of them, they're covered with wool, the wool is used to make cloth, sheep eat grass, their babies are called lambs.)

Jesus said that all his followers are like sheep, and He is like a shepherd. Does that mean we have wool on our skin and we eat grass? Does that mean that Jesus walks around us with a shepherd's staff?

When Jesus said his followers are like sheep and He is the shepherd, He meant He takes care of us the same way a shepherd takes care of his flock. Jesus gives us what we need each day- food, clothes, a house to live in – just like the shepherd. The shepherd provides the sheep with a place to sleep at night and takes them to places where there is plenty of water and grass.

The shepherd also protects the sheep. Sometimes people want to steal the sheep, so the shepherd watches them closely.

Thieves pretend to be the shepherd and call to the sheep to follow them. Because of these thieves, it is very important that the sheep know the voice of the shepherd. They need to recognize the shepherd's voice and know who is calling them- the shepherd or a thief.

In the Bible, Jesus said that we need to know his voice, just like the sheep need to know the voice of the shepherd. When we know Jesus' voice, we can hear him teaching us how to obey God. We can hear Jesus' voice saying, "I love you and I am always with you," when we are sad or afraid.

How can we learn to hear Jesus' voice? Pray, read the Bible, learn in church and Sunday school. When we pray and take time to listen, we can hear Jesus. In the Bible we can read the words of Jesus and listen to him.

Remember to listen to Jesus every day and follow his voice. He loves us and wants to take care of us.

Prayer: Jesus, thank you for protecting us and taking care of everything we need. Please help us to listen to your voice. Amen.

23. Going On A Trip...John 14:1-3

Do you like to travel? Do you like to go on trips? I especially like trips where I can visit people I love- my parents, my brother, my friends. Do you ever visit your grandparents? What about other family? (Give time for the children to share their experiences.)

Getting ready to go see people we love is exciting too. If they live far away, you probably need to pack a suitcase with all your clothes and a sleeping bag or pillow. You'll need your toothbrush and toothpaste, maybe some special toys and something to play with while you're in the car.

If your grandparents or other family live close by, you still have to get ready to see them. You need to get dressed and put on your shoes. You might need to wash your face or brush your teeth. Getting ready is half the fun or the visit!

There is one person who I love and would like to go see- Jesus. But Jesus doesn't live in another town like my friends. He lives in heaven with God. How can I see Jesus? We are told in the Bible, when we die we will see him.

How can we get ready for our trip to heaven? Do you think we need to pack a suitcase and a special pillow? (Allow for responses.)

We don't need to pack a suitcase, but there are somethings we can do to get ready to see Jesus. The Bible tells us in heaven we'll be singing- so we can learn some Bible songs to practice. We will be talking to God and Jesus – so praying will help us to get ready. We will be praising Jesus; that means telling him how grateful we are for all the wonderful things he has done. So, we can praise him today to get ready.

Most importantly, to get ready to see Jesus in heaven is to believe that he is the son of God. We need to believe he died on the cross to take our punishment for the times we have gone against God's law. We need to ask Jesus to come into our hearts and be our friend forever. He will do all these things if we ask him. Then we will be ready for our big trip to heaven.

Prayer: Jesus, thank you for providing a way for us to be with you forever in heaven. Please help us to be ready to see you. We love you, Jesus. Amen.

24. The Test Of Love...John 14:23-24

Raise your hand if your parents tell you, "Clean up your room." Why do your parents ask you to clean your room? (Give the children time to answer.) If you leave your toys laying around someone might step on one of them; then the toys would be broken. Also, if you don't pick up your toys their pieces might get lost.

Let's think of other reasons why you should obey your parents and pick up your room. If you take care of your toys, your parents may be more agreeable to buy you more. They know that since you take care of what you already have, you will probably take care of something new.

Can you think of any other reasons to clean up your room? (Allow the children to respond.) The best reason of all is love-that's right, love. You will make your parents happy when you pick up your toys. And when you love someone, you like to make them happy. You show your parents you love them by doing what they ask you to do.

(Read John 14:23-24.) Jesus says, "If you love me, you'll do the things I ask you to do." The way we can show Jesus how much we love him is doing what he asks. What are some things Jesus is asking us to do? Some answers could be: love each other, pray, help others in need. When we do these things, we show Jesus how much we love him, and we make him happy, just like when you clean your room or do other things your parents ask.

How can we show Jesus or our parents how much we love them? By doing what they ask us to do.

Prayer: Jesus, thank you for showing love to us. Please help us to obey you and show our love for you. Amen.

25. Growing Grapes...John 15:5

Today I need your help to bring a story to life. You will be the pictures. You do the actions I will show you as I tell the story.

Once there was a beautiful garden that grew grapes. This kind of a garden is called a vineyard. In the vineyard grew a large vine. (Hold your arms out from your sides slightly bent. Tilt your hands and fingers upwards so your arms and hands resemble a vine.)

On that grapevine there were many branches. The grapevine was strong and could hold many branches. The food from the soil went up through the roots (gently shake one leg and then the other to show roots) to the branches on the vine. As the sun shone on the vine (place your arms straight up over your head, then lower your arms slowly as you gently wiggle your fingers to mimic rain falling) the vine sent nourishment to the branches. The vine and the branches grew. (Place your arms again in the shape of a vine and stretch them a little higher to show growth)

Over time, fat grapes grew on the branches. (Place your arms at your sides and stand them out from your body to show roundness.)

One branch was not as big as the others. Its' grapes were small. This branch was sad. (Make your hands into fists close your eyes and turn your hands at the wrists to show crying.)

The little branch said, "I am so small. I'll never be big. I'll never grow fat juicy grapes." The strong vine spoke gently to the small branch and said, "You are smaller than the others now, but if you stay connected to me I'll give you food and water. You will grow and make juicy grapes. If you break away from me, you'll lose your nourishment. You'll wither up and turn brown. Then you'll never grow grapes. Just stay with me and you'll be strong and healthy."

The first person to tell this story of the vine was Jesus. When he told this story, he wasn't giving gardening lessons. He was teaching about himself and his followers. What do you think this story means? (Allow for responses.)

(Read John 15:5.) In this story Jesus is telling us that if we want to do special work for God, we have to stay close to Him. How can we stay close to Jesus? (Give time for children to answer.) We can pray, read our Bibles, and come to worship.

Have you ever sat in church and thought, "I'm just a kid? I'll never do anything special for God." Have you every felt like a small branch in the story? (Allow children to share their feelings.)

Jesus said if we stay close to him we will bear fruit, no matter how old we are. Does that mean if we pray and read our Bibles we'll grow grapes out of our fingers? When Jesus said we would bear fruit He meant our lives and our actions would please God. When we bear fruit for God we do good things for Him in this world. Let's all stay connected to Jesus, so we can grow strong in Him and work for his Kingdom.

Prayer: Jesus, thank you for helping us grow. Please help us to stay close to you. Amen.

26. Questions...John 20:24-29

Do you ever ask your parents or your teachers questions? Do you have questions about the things God has made? If you had one question to ask God, what would it be? (Allow for the children to respond.)

A man named Thomas had lots of questions to ask Jesus. We can read about him in the Bible. Thomas was one of Jesus' followers, he was Jesus' friend. But he wasn't around when the disciples discovered that Jesus was alive on Easter. So, Thomas has questions: how did they know Jesus was alive? How did he come back to life?

Jesus came to Thomas and answered his questions. Jesus showed him the wounds He had from the nails that held Him to the cross. He showed Thomas that He was alive! And Thomas believed!

There are some questions that are easy to answer. Some other questions we have are more difficult. We may not know some answers until we get to heaven and can ask Jesus face to face. Let's be thankful that God gave us curious minds to wonder and ask questions. Let's be thankful that God loves us and isn't angry when we have questions. Let's be thankful that whether we get the answers to our questions now or in heaven, we know that God knows everything and has all the answers to our questions.

Prayer: Jesus, thank you for our minds to think, wonder, and ask questions. Please help us to trust you as we ask questions. Thank you for your wisdom. Amen.

27. What If I Mess Up?...John 21:15-17

Can you tell me the names of some of Jesus' friends, the disciples? (Allow for responses.) One of the disciples we read about many times in the Bible is Peter. There are many stories in the Bible about Peter. When the Holy Spirit came to the believers Peter became a strong speaker who carried the message of Jesus to many people.

Let's pretend we are going to tell someone about Peter. We know he is a good friend of Jesus, and he was a powerful preacher. Let's think of words that might describe Peter. If you think he was peaceful, raise your hand. If you think he made good choices, raise your hand. If you think he always told the truth raise your hand. Allow for children to raise their hands after each question.

Normally when we think of someone who is in the Bible, and who was a disciple, we think they would always make good choices and be peaceful and truthful. But before the Holy Spirit came to the disciples, Peter didn't do any of these things!

I'll tell you a few stories about Peter. If you think he's making a good choice in the story, say "Yes!" If you think he's making a bad choice say "No!"

In the first story we see Peter when the soldiers have come to arrest Jesus and take him away to be crucified. Peter is with Jesus. Peter takes his sword and cuts off the ear of one of the men who have come for Jesus. Was this a good choice? Pause to allow the children to answer.

After Jesus was arrested, Peter followed the soldiers to the place where Jesus was taken. When he went inside to be near Jesus, a girl standing in the doorway asked Peter, "Are you one of Jesus' disciples?" Peter lied and said, "No." Was that a good choice?

While the religious leaders were questioning Jesus, Peter was waiting outside. Again, someone asked him, "Are you one of Jesus' followers?" Again Peter lied and said, "No." Was that a good choice?

As you can see, Peter didn't always tell the truth. He wasn't always peaceful. He didn't always make good choices. Are you always peaceful or truthful? Do you always make good decisions?

No one except Jesus ever lived a perfect life. Everyone has done something to make God sad, just like Peter.

But Jesus forgave Peter. After Jesus came back to life, he talked to Peter and gave him special instructions. Read John 21:15-17. When Jesus told Peter to "feed my sheep" Jesus was instructing Peter to tell others about Jesus.

Jesus loved Peter. We all make mistakes. But Jesus loves us too. We can tell Jesus we are sorry. We can turn away from doing the things that make God sad. We can turn back to God and do great work for him with his power – just like Peter.

Prayer: God, thank you that you love us even when we mess up. Please help us to turn you and say we're sorry. Thank you for forgiving us. Amen.

28. Be a Barnabas! ...Acts 9:19b-28

In the early days of Christianity, after Jesus had gone back to heaven, the disciples traveled around, telling everyone about Jesus. Some people didn't like what the disciples were saying and had them put in jail. Or killed.

One of those people was a man named Saul. Saul tracked down Christians and had them jailed or put to death. One day when Saul was traveling to find more Christians, Jesus appeared to him in a light so bright it made Saul go blind. Saul's friends helped him on to the next city. While Saul was there, a Christian came to the place where he stayed, prayed with Saul, and God healed Saul's eyes.

After that, Saul became a Christian. He changed his name to Paul, and told everyone about how he had met Jesus. Many people believed in Jesus because of Saul, now Paul. Have you ever been like Paul, changing from doing something wrong to living God's way? (Allow for responses.)

The disciples and some Christians were afraid of Paul. They remembered how he had hurt Christians. They didn't want to be around Paul. They didn't believe he had become a Christian. What would you have done if you had been one of those early disciples? Would you have believed Paul and his story? (Give time for the children to respond.)

There was one Christian, a man named Barnabas, who believed Paul. He became Paul's friend. He forgave Paul. Barnabas took Paul to the disciples and convinced them Paul had changed. The disciples believed Barnabas and accepted Paul. Paul became a great leader among Christians and led many people to Jesus. Many of his letters and teachings are in the Bible today.

I wonder what would have happened to Paul if Barnabas had not helped him. Do you think the disciples would have accepted Paul? (Allow for responses.)

Let's pretend you are playing with your friends and one person cheats in the game. Now everyone is upset with them and no one wants to play with them. Even after that person who cheated says they are sorry and promises to play by the rules, your friends won't include them back into the game.

Would you be a Barnabas and stand with your friend? Could you forgive them and help them get back in the game again?

God wants us to forgive each other, just as the disciples forgave Paul. Forgiving each other is a great way to show Jesus' love for others and be a good friend.

Prayer: God, please help us to forgive each other. Please help us to be loving and brave, like Barnabas. Help us to show your love to each other. Amen.

29. Live in Peace...Romans 12:17-21

A girl named Anna was playing on the playground at school with some friends. The friends were swinging on the monkey bars. When Anna tried to pull herself along the monkey bars she fell. She tried and tried, but her arms weren't strong enough to hold her up.

When she fell, the other girls laughed at her. They called her names. This hurt Anna's feelings.

She wanted to call them names right back. She even thought about hitting or pushing the girls. Do you think hurting the girls or using unkind words would help Anna? Do you think that would make Jesus happy? (Allow for the children to respond)

Let's see if the Bible has any instructions for Anna. (Read Romans 12:17-21.) What does "repay...evil for evil... "mean? (Give time for the children to share their ideas.) When someone does something bad to us, we should not hurt them in return.

Why is "...repaying evil for evil..." a bad idea? (Some responses could be: If Anna calls names or hurts one of the other girls they may start an even bigger fight; someone may get hurt; they would get in trouble with the teacher.)

What does the Bible tell Anna to do in this situation? Be kind to your enemies; do your best to live in peace. If you knew Anna, what would you tell her to do? Tell the girls to stop calling her names, walk away.

Anna could use words to tell others how she feels. Anna might need to find better friends to play with- friends who will be kind and not hurtful.

Either way, it's important for Anna and us to learn that when someone hurts us, hurting them back is never a good idea.

Prayer: God, thank you for friends who love us. Help us to find good friends. Help us to solve our problems in ways that make you happy. Amen.

30. Angry Feelings…Ephesians 4:26

Raise your hand and tell me one thing that makes you angry. What do you do when you get angry? Do you think God is happy when He sees how you act when you're angry? (Allow for responses to each question.)

(Read Ephesians 4:26.) Does this verse say getting angry is wrong? No – this verse says when we have angry feelings inside of us we shouldn't sin. Everyone gets angry from time to time. Our problems come when we make bad choices in acting out our feelings.

Part of this verse says, "In your anger do not sin…" What is sin? Sin is when we make God sad or break one of his laws. When we're angry we shouldn't break God's laws. When we're angry it is wrong to destroy someone's property or hit someone or use rude words. Those actions break God's laws of loving each other and respecting each other.

We also learn from this verse, "Do not let the sun go down while you are still angry…" What do you think that means? Allow for responses. When you are angry, don't hold those feelings inside you. Find ways to get those feelings out.

If it's wrong to call someone names or hurt someone when we are angry, then what can we do to get those feelings out? (Some responses include: count to 10, take a deep breath, go somewhere to be alone and calm down, pray, think about something peaceful, and talk to someone you trust.) When we are angry, we have many good behavior choices we can make.

When we feel angry we can turn to God and ask for his help to make good choices in what we say and do.

Prayer: God, thank you for our feelings. Please help us to make you happy in how we act out our feelings. Please make us strong to make good choice when we are angry. Amen.

31. Why Should I Obey My Parents?...Ephesians 6:1-3, Exodus 20:12

Once there was a family with three children named Jacob, Ruth, and Samuel. To Jacob, Ruth and Samuel it seemed their parents were very strict. Do you know what that means? Their parents gave the family a lot of rules, and everyone in the family was expected to follow those rules. Some of the family rules were: don't call people names, don't hit or hurt each other, and when you go out to play always tell Mom or Dad where you are going.

Mom and Dad also made rules about homework. Jacob, Ruth, and Samuel had to have their homework finished before they could watch television in the evening. Dad and Mom helped them get ready for tests and they read together at night.

Jacob, Ruth, and Samuel thought their family had a lot of rules. Does your family have any rules? Raise your hand and tell me one of your family's rules. (Allow for responses.)

Jacob, Ruth, and Samuel wondered why there were so many rules in their family. Then one day at school Jacob had a test in Math. The test was very challenging, but he remembered the times he had worked on this math homework with his mom. He remembered the math facts he had learned with his mom's help, and Jacob was able to finish the test with a good grade.

The next afternoon Ruth was outside with her friends. They wanted her to go with them down the street to explore the woods at the end of the neighborhood. Ruth remembered the family rule – "Always tell someone where you are going when you are playing outside". When she asked her Dad about exploring the woods he reminded her about poison ivy that grew there. Ruth decided to stay away from the woods. The next day her friends who went to the woods to explore were itchy and red and uncomfortable with a poison ivy rash.

A few days later Samuel was playing at recess with his friends. A few of his friends got angry with each other and a fight started. Samuel remembered his family's rules- "Don't call each other names. Don't hit or hurt each other" Samuel stayed out of the fight. When someone told the teachers they came to stop the fight, the other kids who were involved had to go the principal's office, but Samuel got to stay out on the playground and have fun.

When Jacob, Ruth, and Samuel obeyed their parent's rules they were safe. They kept out of trouble. They learned following family rules taught them well. Read Ephesians 6:1-3. What do you think the Bible is teaching us in these verses? (Give time for the children's answers.)

Obeying your parents and honoring your father and mother means you remember what they have taught you. You obey your family's rules. Then you will be successful, safe, and happy.

How do your family rules help you? (Allow for answers.) Let's pray and ask God for help in following family rules and obeying our parents.

Prayer: God, thank you for our parents. Please help them to be wise in leading our families and making the rules. Please help us to honor our parents and obey their rules. Amen.

32. When Should I Pray? ...1 Thessalonians 5:17

(Several specific children's names are used in the children's sermon today. If you have children in your group who have these same names, consider substituting their names for another so they won't feel singled out.)

(After each scenario the children are instructed to stand up. Have them briefly stand, and then sit down again to hear the next part of the story.)

Today we are going to hear about some kids who love God just like you. These kids need help solving problems. Let's see if we can help them.

First, I have friend named Ashley, Ashley has been visiting church with one of her friends. She likes what she is learning, and she is having fun in church. But Ashley doesn't know much about God. She wants to know God better. If you think that praying and talking to God is a good way Ashley can get to know him better, please stand up.

I have another friend who needs your help. His name is William. William has been going to church for a while. He has made some friends there. He also has friends who don't go to church. Those friends who don't go to church have formed a secret club. They want William to be a part of it. To join the club, you must steal something from a store and bring it to the club meeting. William has learned in church that stealing is wrong, but he wants to be friends with the kids in the club. William needs someone to guide him when he doesn't know what to do. If you think praying and asking God for guidance would help William, please stand up.

Jillian is another friend of mine. Jillian's dad is a police officer. Whenever he goes to work, Jillian worries about him. She knows his job can be dangerous. She wants him to be safe. If you think Jillian can pray and tell her worries to God, stand up.

Another friend of mine is named Logan. Logan has been working to learn his math problems for a test in school. He takes the test and then waits for the teacher to check it for mistakes. When he gets the test from the teacher, Logan sees he answered almost all the questions correctly. The teacher tells him he did a good job. Logan is so happy! If you think Logan can pray and say thank you to God for helping him study and do well on the test, stand up.

Another friend of mine is Casey. Casey got into a fight with her younger sister. She called her names and hit her. Now she feels badly about what she did. If you think Casey can pray and tell God she's sorry, stand up.

If you thought all my friends could pray about their life situations, you were right! We can pray about anything, at any time. (Read 1 Thessalonians 5:17.) The Bible tells us to pray all the time. God loves us. He wants us to always talk and listen to him.

Prayer: God, thank you for loving us. Please help us to remember to always talk to you. Thank you that we can pray to you any time. Amen.

33. Healthy Body, Healthy Spirit...1Timothy 4:8

Today I need your help. I want to develop a plan to keep my body healthy. What do I need to do? (Possible answers include: Eat veggies and fruits, exercise, get plenty of sleep.) You know a lot about keeping your body healthy! Why is it important to keep our bodies healthy? We can live longer; we will have energy to play and go to school, we will not be sick as often

You have been very helpful with my plan to keep my body healthy. No, I need another plan. Can you help me have a healthy spirit? How would I do that? Pray, read your Bible, go to church, help others, tell others about Jesus. Why is having a healthy spirit so important? A healthy spirit makes God happy.

Which do you think is more important, a healthy body or a healthy spirit? (Allow for responses.)

The Bible has an answer to that question. Read 1 Timothy 4:8. The Bible tells us a healthy spirit is more important. The verse says that a healthy spirit will help us now while we live, to do the things that make God happy. A healthy spirit will also help us when we die; with a healthy spirit we will live forever with God in heaven. A healthy body is good, but eventually everyone's body will become old and worn out. We need a healthy spirit not only for this life, but also for our forever life with God.

When we take time to exercise or eat vegetables and fruits, we also should take time to pray, read our Bibles, and spend time with Christian friends at church.

Prayer: God, thank you for the wisdom of the Bible. Help us to work for healthy bodies and healthy spirits. Amen.

34. Changes...Hebrews 13:8

I've been thinking about changes. Have you ever heard the saying, "Everything changes?" What can you think of that changes? (Allow for responses.) The weather changes all the time. People change, growing from babies to children to adults. The seasons change from spring to summer and fall to winter. We even change our clothes every day.

Do you like it when things change? (Give time for the children to answer.) Sometimes change is happy, like when you get new shoes because your feet have grown. Some change is sad, like when a friend moves away.

We said that everything changes, but I know something that doesn't change. It's a person; the Bible tells us that Jesus will be the same yesterday, today, and forever. We can count on Jesus to love us and forgive us forever. Jesus will always be there to help us make good choices and live in a way that makes God happy. Jesus will never leave us nor stop loving us.

Prayer: Jesus, thank you that you are always there for us. Thank you that you never change. Help us to rest in your never changing love for us. Amen.

35. Showing What You Believe...James 2:14-17

(Begin by telling the children this story. If you have children in the group with these or similar names of the children in the story, please substitute them with other names so the children in your group will not feel singled out or uncomfortable.)

Rebecca and James went to church every week. They always sat quietly for the children's moments and they knew all the correct answers to the questions. They knew many Bible stories and all the Ten Commandments.

On Monday morning at school, one of Rebecca's friends whispered to her, "At recess we're going to make a club, but we're not going to let Melanie in the club."

Later that day at recess, Rebecca saw Melanie all alone looking very sad. Rebecca ran off with the new girl's club and was glad that she was included.

The same day James went to play with his friends in the neighborhood after school. The guys decided it would be fun to steal vegetables from Mrs. Reed's garden while she was at work. James laughed at the boys as they ran through the rows of vegetables, storming the tall ears of corn into the ground. Then he joined in when they threw tomatoes at each other.

The next time Rebecca and James went to church the Bible story was about loving your neighbor. Both Rebecca and James sat right in the front and answered all the questions correctly.

How does this story make you feel? (Allow for responses.) Rebecca and James knew all the right answers when the teachers in church asked them. Did Rebecca and James follow that teaching when they were with their friends away from church?

Someone who doesn't know a lot about church may look at Rebecca and James's behavior and say, "If that's how the Bible teaches a person to act, I don't want to read it!"

(Read James 2:14-17.) How would this verse help Rebecca and James? (Allow for responses.) We show our faith - what we believe - more by what we do than what we say. Knowing the Bible is important, but putting what we learn into action is the best way to show Jesus to the world and to share His love with others.

Prayer: God, thank you for the Bible and all you teach us. Please help us to remember what we learn in church. Please help us to put what we learn into action in our lives every day. Amen.

36. Mouth on Fire...James 3:5

Have you ever seen a fire in a fireplace or a campfire? Have you ever seen a fire on television? (Allow for responses.)

If you have ever seen pictures of a forest fire on television you might have heard how the fire started. Sometimes the fire starts from lightning, but often the fire begins with a careless person throwing down a lit cigarette or leaving a campfire before it's put out. On dry leaves or grass the fire can start and spread quickly.

Did you know that the Bible says your tongue is like a fire? (Read James 3:5.) What do you think that means?

Let's imagine you are on the playground at school with your friends. You are playing and having fun, then someone gets mad and says some angry words at someone else. That friend then says something rude back. Before you know it, those two are yelling at each other. Soon some other friends start yelling, maybe even fighting. Now everyone is angry, and no one wants to have fun.

In thinking back, what started the fight? (Allow for responses.) Angry words from just one person started the fight. Just like one careless campfire in the woods starts a forest fire, just one angry word from one person can turn the whole playground into a battleground.

The words from our mouths are very powerful. Kind words can make people feel happy, calm, and confident. Unkind words bring hurt, sadness, and fear.

You are very careful with fire. You should never play with fire or matches because fire is very dangerous. Please try to be careful with your words just like you are careful with fire.

Prayer: Jesus, thank you for words and for the good they bring to us. Please help us to be careful with words. Please help us to use our words for good. Amen.

37. When I Am Afraid...1 Peter 5:7

(Have the children sit far enough away from each other to have room to move.) Say, "Today I need your help to tell our story. I will tell the Bible story and act out some of the words. You can help me tell the story by copying my motions that go along with the words of the story."

In the Bible we read a true story about a prophet of God named Elijah. (Hold hands in the shape of a book.) Elijah was a very brave man. (Hands on hips, chest out in a "Superman" pose.) Elijah lived at time when the king and queen of Israel were disobeying God. The king and queen were worshiping idols. They were praying to statues and not the one true God. This king and queen also led people to worship those fake gods. (Arms straight up over head, then bow down at the waist.)

God told Elijah to tell the king and queen they were disobeying God. God helped Elijah turn the people back to worshiping him. This made the king and queen angry. (Arms folded across chest, eyebrows furrowed.) The queen told Elijah she wanted to kill him. Elijah was afraid, and he ran away. (Run in place; in a sitting position, the children can stomp their feet.)

Also in our Bibles we can read the true story of a man named David. (Hold hands in the shape of a book.) In David's time a man named Saul was the king of Israel. (Hold hands on head with fingertips touching in the shape of a circle to form a crown.) But Saul had disobeyed God many times, and God told him he couldn't be king anymore. (Shake your head "no"). God chose David to be the new king. (Hold hands on head with fingertips touching in the shape of a circle to form a crown.) This made Saul angry, and he wanted to kill David. David and his friends ran away. (Run in place; in a sitting position, the children can stomp their feet.)

Another true story in the Bible is about a woman named Esther. (Hold hands in the shape of a book.) Esther was a Jewish woman. She lived during a time when God's people, the Jews, were scattered away from Israel, living in other parts of the world. (Hands over eyes to shade them, look around the room as if you were searching for something far away.) Esther and the Jews were living in a country called Persia. Esther was so beautiful that the king of Persia picked her to be queen. (Hold hands on head with fingertips touching in the shape of a circle to form a crown.) While she was queen, Esther found out a very bad man wanted to destroy the Jews living in Persia. Esther knew she had to help her people, but she was afraid. (Open hands on face, eyes wide open to look afraid.)

In all these stories we learn about people who loved God and faced times when they were afraid. We are all afraid sometimes, just like Elijah, David, and Esther. Just like them, we may want to run away. But they also did something else when they were afraid. They prayed, told God their fears, and asked God for help. And God helped them.

When Elijah prayed, God sent people to help him. When David prayed God kept him safe until Saul died and David was made king. When Esther prayed God made her brave and wise to tell the king about the plan to kill the Jews. The king stopped the plan, and Esther and all her people were safe.

(Read 1 Peter 5:7.) We can give all our cares, fears, and worries to God because he loves us. He is always watching over us.

Prayer: God, thank you that you are always watching over us. Please help us to pray to you when we are afraid. Amen.

For Special Days

38. Do Over!...New Year's Day...1 John 1:9

Let's pretend you are playing baseball with friends. Get ready. Grab a bat. (Pretend to hold a baseball bat. Have the children do the same.) Imagine the pitcher is throwing the ball. Here comes the ball. Give a good swing. (Swing your imaginary bat). Say, "Oh, man! We missed the ball!"

What can you do? Some players might say "Do over!" When you're playing with your friends do you ever call a do over? Do you know what that means? (Allow the children to explain.) A "do over" means if you're playing a game and something goes wrong, it's not counted against you or your team. You can take your turn again. You can do it over.

Let's think about another time when you are playing baseball with your friends. Your team is winning. Some kids in your team start making fun of the other team because they are losing. You want to be a part of the group, so you call the other team names too.

Later you think about what happened. You feel bad about what you have done. You know your words made the other team and God sad. You want to tell God you're sorry. Can you have a "do over" with God?

(Read John 1:9.) The Bible tells us that if we confess - if we tell God what we did and turn away from our wrong actions - God will forgive us and make our hearts clean.

A holiday is coming (or has just passed). That holiday is New Year's Day. On New Year's Day many people make plans to change their actions and live better lives. On New Year's Day they want a "do over".

As a part of God's family, we can have a "do over" any time we want! All we need to do is pray and ask God to forgive us. Then we can turn away from those actions that made God sad. With God's power we can have a "do over" and live in ways that please God.

Prayer: God, thank you for forgiving us when we confess and pray to you. Please help us to live in ways that make you happy. Amen.

39. One Family...Martin Luther King, Jr. Day... Galatians 3:28

(As you ask each question, give time for the children to respond. Be mindful of shy children who have something to say, but who may hesitate. Include everyone in the conversation.)

Do you like to eat different foods? What unusual foods have you tried lately?

On vacation days do you like to visit a place where you have never been? What new place would you like to visit?

Have you ever come home from school and found your parents have cleaned and rearranged your room? Do you like changes?

Do you like to meet new people? Have you ever met someone who wears their hair in a special way or talks different from you?

Some people don't like food that is unusual. Some people don't like people who are different from them. Why do you think that is? They may be afraid. They might be embarrassed because they don't know how to act in a new situation with new people.

This month we are remembering the life of a famous man. Dr. Martin Luther King, Jr. We remember him because he worked for many years to help people to see past the differences in each other. He wanted everyone, no matter what they looked like or where they came from, to be equal.

(Read Galatians 3:28.) What do you think this verse means? We may come from a variety of places or have different jobs, but Jesus came to the earth for everyone. Jesus died on the cross for all people. When we are followers of Jesus, we are all in God's family together.

Prayer: God, thank you for sending Jesus to the earth for all of us. Thank you that you love everyone, no matter what color their hair or what language they speak. Please help us to reach out to all people, even those who are different from us. Help us show your love to everyone. Amen.

40. Leaders ...President's Day...1 Peter 2:13-17

Tell me the name of your favorite teacher. Why is that person your favorite teacher? (Give each child a chance to respond.)

Have you ever thought about teachers being leaders? What is a leader? They are the boss, the one in charge. Your teachers are leaders in school.

Can you think of other leaders? They are coaches, scout leaders, parents, Sunday school teachers, government officials. This time of year, we think about leaders. One of the special days we celebrate this month is President's Day. On President's Day we remember George Washington and Abraham Lincoln, two men who were presidents - leaders - of our country.

Usually we don't get to work with the President, but there are other leaders we work with every week: teachers, coaches, scout leaders, and parents. How do you act toward those leaders? Are you respectful of your leaders? Are you helpful and obedient? (Allow for responses.)

Did you know that the Bible teaches us how we should act toward leaders? (Read 1 Peter 2:13-17.) These words were written by a disciple of Jesus named Peter. He wrote to some Christians who were led by a king. We don't live in a country ruled by a king, but we can still follow Peter's directions.

Peter tells us we should respect our leaders. When we show respect to leaders, people around us will see the way Christians live - with love and kindness. Peter tells us to love Christians, respect leaders, and worship God above all. How can we show respect for our leaders? Listen when they are talking, follow their advice, and talk to them and about them with kind words.

We should also pray for our leaders - our coaches, teachers, parents, and leaders in government - and ask God to help them look to him to guide them in all things. We can pray God will help them to be good leaders.

Prayer: Thank you God, for our leaders. Please help them to follow you in all the decisions they make. Help us to respect our leaders and serve you always. Amen.

41. Visible Love...Valentine's Day...1 John 4: 11-12

Have you ever heard the story of "The Invisible Man"? The story tells about a man who drinks a special potion and he becomes invisible.

What does "visible" mean? What does "invisible" mean? (Allow for responses.)

What are some things that are visible? (Give time for each child to answer.) What are some things that are invisible? (Air, wind, or God.) How do you know that air is there, if we can't see it? When we breathe we can feel it; we can see the wind moving in the trees.

How do you know God is there, even if you can't see him? The Bible gives us an answer to this question. (Read John 4:11-12.) When we love each other, the world can see God. How does this work? How can loving each other make the invisible visible?

How do we show love to each other? (Some responses could be: giving hugs, sharing, listening to each other, saying kind words, helping each other.) How do these actions show God to the world?

Let's think about one way of showing love; listening to each other. Suppose your friend went on a great vacation, and they wanted to tell you about it. Listening to them might not be very exciting. Listening to them might make you jealous that you didn't go on a great vacation. But listening to your friend tells them you think they are important. Your friend feels good when they can talk to you. Your friend may ask you, "Why are you being so nice to me?"

Then you can tell them what you have learned about God. You can tell them how much God loves us and how Christians show God's love to others. Ta Da! When you showed love and listened to others, you helped them see God!

Showing love does more than make us feel good. Showing love is more than giving Valentines or candy on Valentine's Day. Showing love makes the invisible God visible to the world around us.

Prayer: God, thank you for loving us. Thank you for the Bible to teach us how to love each other. Please help us to show the invisible you to others when we love them. Amen.

42. Leprechaun Gold!...St. Patrick's Day...Psalm 119:72

A special day is coming up this month called "Saint Patrick's Day". Do you know anything about that day? (Allow for responses.) When many people think about Saint Patrick's Day they think about leprechauns and gold. The old stories tell us that leprechauns are little magic people who have pots of gold. The stories say if you catch a leprechaun, they must give you their gold.

We know those stories aren't true, but we can have fun thinking about them. I was thinking especially about the pot of gold that the leprechaun would give me if I caught him. What would you do if you had a pot of gold? (Some children might say they would buy toys or new clothes, cars, or houses.) Having a pot of gold sounds like it would be wonderful! Having a pot of gold might make you happy. When you buy new toys, cars, clothes, or a house you'll feel happy for a time.

But one day those toys will get old. You'll get tired of them. You'll grow up and won't like those old toys. The cars you buy will eventually get old and worn out. You'll outgrow the clothes you buy. Even houses eventually get old and run down. Everything that people can buy with gold will, sooner or later, fade away or break or wear out. Then the happiness goes away too.

Did you know that the Bible talks about gold, too? It doesn't mention any leprechauns but here is what it says: "The law from God's mouth is more precious to me than thousands of pieces of silver and gold." (Psalm 119:72 NIV)

Let's think about God's law. What does God's law teach us? Love each other, pray, read the Bible, give to others. One important teaching is to love God and love others. How do we act when we show love to God? Pray, give, study the Bible. How do we act when we show love to others? Share, listen, and help each other.

Reading the Bible doesn't break like a toy. Helping each other doesn't get worn out like a new pair of blue jeans. Sharing with others doesn't break down like a car.

What we learn from God's law will last forever. What we buy with gold will eventually fall apart or wear out. The Bible really is true when it says that God's law is more precious than gold or silver - even the gold from a leprechaun!

Prayer: God, thank you that what we learn from the bible will never wear out. Thank you that what we do for you will never break or get old. Please forgive us when we focus on things that don't last. Help us live for what will last. Amen.

43. Telling the Truth...April Fool's Day...Ephesians 4:25, Hebrews 6:18

An especially fun day is celebrated on the first day of April. Do you know what day that is? Do you play April Fool's tricks on your friends? What are your favorite tricks? (Allow time for each child to respond.)

Many of the tricks I've seen try to make someone believe something that isn't true. On April Fool's Day I walk around very carefully, and I don't believe anything anyone tells me!

Playing tricks or twisting the truth on April Fool's Day is fun, but what would happen if you played practical jokes on your friends every day? What if you told lies all the time? How would your friends and family treat you? (Give time for the children to answer.)

(Read Ephesians 4:25.) Because we are all members of God's family we should be able to trust each other. When we make telling lies a habit, we break that trust.

We should also tell the truth because we want to be like God; God always tells the truth. The Bible tells us that God does not lie. We can believe everything He says. When He tells us He loves us, we can believe it. When God tells us we are forgiven because of Jesus's death on the cross, we can believe it. When God says we will live with Him forever in heaven, we can believe it. Those are not April Fool's jokes!

Prayer: God, thank you for fun times with family and friends. Thank you that you always tell us the truth. Help us to be truthful with others. Amen.

4/13/25

44. Praises!...Palm Sunday...John 12:12-13

Raise your hand if you can tell me what we are celebrating today. (Allow for answers.)

Palm Sunday is the day we remember when Jesus rode into Jerusalem on a donkey. The people of the city celebrated and praised God.

Some people celebrated by waving palm branches. Some people shouted. They all praised God.

Today on Palm Sunday we can do the same thing! Today we praise God. We thank him for sending Jesus to be with us. What are some ways we can praise God? We can do it through singing or in prayer.

The Bible says we can praise God by raising our hands. Let's all raise our hands and say, "Praise God!" (Have the children raise their hands, wave their arms, maybe wiggle their fingers.) We can praise God by clapping our hands. Have the children clap their hands and say, "Praise God!" We can shout our praises. On the count of three, let's all shout "Praise God!" (Lead the children in a shout.) Or we can whisper our praises. (Lead the children in whispering, "Praise God!")

There are many ways to praise God. Let's remember to always praise God for all the wonderful things he has done, especially for sending Jesus to us.

Prayer: God, thank you for sending Jesus to us to save us and teach us your ways. Please help us to praise you every day. Amen.

45. Surprises!...Easter....Luke 24:1- 12

Do you like surprises? I do. A surprise is when something happens you didn't expect. There are good surprises and bad surprises. Can you think of a good surprise? What's a bad surprise? (Allow for responses following each question.)

Easter is a time full of surprises. During Easter time we go on Easter egg hunts to find eggs with candy surprises inside. Did you get surprised with an Easter basket this morning? What kind of surprises are in Easter baskets? (Give time for the children to share their experiences.)

Surprises are all around at Easter. When we read in our Bibles about Easter, we find surprises there too, some of these surprises are good, some are bad. I'm sure the disciples were surprised when the Roman soldiers arrested Jesus and put him on a cross to die. That surprise was very sad.

But the Easter story also has the best surprise ever. Do you know what that surprise was? Jesus came back to life! He died on the cross and was buried in a tomb. But God's power brought him back to life! When some of Jesus's friends went to the tomb, an angel there told them Jesus was alive. I'm sure those friends were surprised.

When Jesus died on the cross he took our punishment for the times we go against the laws of God. When he came back to life, he opened the way for us to be with Him and God forever in heaven when we die. Jesus coming back to life is the best surprise of all - on Easter and all year long!

Prayer: Jesus, thank you for Easter. Thank you for opening the way for us to be with you in heaven. Thank you for good surprises. Amen.

46. Growing Flowers of Praise...Spring Time... Psalm 147:7-8; James 1:17

Which season is your favorite? Why? (Allow for answers.) Some children may choose a favorite season because of their birthday, vacations or Christmas.

We can think of something wonderful in every time of the year. We may even get presents during some of those special times. When you receive a present from someone, what should you say to that person? "Thank you."

Have you ever thought all those wonderful occasions you named are all like gifts? I don't mean that a vacation must come in a box with a ribbon on it. I mean that your family, the money to pay for the vacation, the beach or wherever you go - everything about that special time - was given to you. You didn't do anything of yourself to make it. Some people call these gifts "blessings".

Who gives us all these great gifts we mentioned? The Bible tells us, "Every good and perfect gift is from above..." (James 1:17 NIV) all those favorite happenings and people are all gifts from God. What should we say when God gives us a gift? "Thank you."

So, let's take time to say, "Thank you" to God. Since we started out talking about the seasons, let's think about the season we are in right now- spring. Flowers bloom in the spring. Today we will be flowers of thanks. When I come around with my pretend rain cloud to rain on you, you will be a flower and bloom - stand up where you are. When you bloom, think of one good gift God has given you and tell God "Thank you" for it.

(Walk around to each child with your hands in fists to make a rain cloud. Hold your fists over their head, then open your fists and wiggle your fingers to mimic rain. Each child will, in turn, stand and say a one sentence "thank you" prayer to God. After they say their sentence, they will sit back down, and another child will have a turn. After every child who wants to participate has had a turn, then you close in prayer. Begin by saying your own "Thank you" prayer.)

Prayer: God, we love you. All your gifts to us are amazing! Help us to remember to say, "Thank you" for all the blessings you send to us. Amen.

47. Promises…Pentecost...John 14:15-17; Acts 2:14-18

Today we're going to talk together about promises. What is a promise? What does it mean when someone makes a promise? How many of you make promises? Do you keep your promises? Do other people make promises to you? Do they keep their promises?(Give the children a chance to share their answers.)

Let's play a game to think about making and keeping promises. I'll name some people who make promises. If this person always keeps their promise, you give me a "thumbs up" sign. (Make a fist, then hold your thumb straight up from the fist.) If the people I name sometimes keep their promises, you show me a "thumbs sideways." (Turn your "thumbs up sign" sideways so your thumb is sticking out from the side.) If this person never keeps their promises, give me a "thumbs down" sign. (Turn the "Thumbs up" sign down so your thumb is pointing down.)

Are you ready? Here we go. (List significant people in the children's life. Some could be: mom, dad, grandparents, brothers, sisters, friends, teachers. Allow for children to respond to each name. At the end, be sure to include themselves. Lastly, name Jesus.)

Today we celebrate Pentecost. Does anyone know why we are celebrating Pentecost? Pentecost is the day Jesus kept one of his promises. Jesus promised the disciples that after he went up to heaven, he would send God's Spirit, called the Holy Spirit, to be with the disciples and help them. On Pentecost, Jesus kept his promise and the Holy Spirit came to the disciples.

Do you know Jesus makes the same promise of the Holy Spirit to us? Jesus promised us God's Spirit would help everyone who wants to follow God's commands. Jesus keeps his promise even today.

Can you think of other promises Jesus has made? (Some responses include: to be with us always; to help us when we are afraid; to show us how to obey God; to take us to heaven when we die.) Does Jesus keep his promises? Yes! Jesus keeps every promise he has ever made – not just some of them, but all of them. You can trust what Jesus says because he always keeps his promises.

Prayer: Jesus, thank you that we can trust you to always keep your promises. Thank you for sending the Holy Spirit to the disciples on Pentecost. Thank you for sending the Holy Spirit to us today. Amen.

48. Light ...First Day of Summer...Matthew 5:14-16

The first day of summer is coming soon (or has just passed). This day is called the Summer Solstice. Does anyone know what that means? (Allow for answers.) The summer solstice is the day when the sun is up in the sky longer than any other day of the year.

Why is light so important to us? (Some responses could be: sunlight helps plants grow, gives heat and solar power, and helps us see.)

Did you know the Bible says we are light? (Read Matthew 5:14-16.) Does this teaching of Jesus mean we give off heat and help plants grow? What do you think it means? (Give time for the children to share their thoughts.)

When people make bad choices, and do things that make God sad it's like they bring darkness into the world. When we do things to make God happy and make good choices we bring light into the world.

When we say something kind we bring the light of Jesus' love into the world. When we share we bring the light of Jesus' love into the world. When we choose to take a deep breath and not fight when we are angry we bring the light of Jesus' love into the world.

On summer days when you see the sun, remember Jesus said we are lights. Remember we are told to take his light into the world.

Prayer: Jesus thank you for the sun and the light it gives us. Thank you for coming to earth and bringing your light. Please help us to also be lights. Help us do the things that make God happy and show your light to others. Amen.

49. Time...A Back to School Message...Psalm 31:15a

The "going back to school" season has started. The summer is over and your family talks about school. You may hear your family talk a lot about time. Since school has started you have to go to bed on time, so you can wake up on time, to be at school on time. And after school you have music lessons or sports practice that take time. Each activity starts at a certain time and ends at a certain time.

For many of us, we have so many things to do we feel like we don't have enough time to get it all finished. Do you feel that you are always in a hurry? Always rushing? (Give each child who has a response a time to share.) Sometimes I feel that way. There never seems to be enough time to do the things we want to do.

Maybe all this rushing makes us tired. Maybe we feel sad that we don't get to do the things we want to do because we don't have time. Maybe we are scared that our families won't have time for us because they are busy too.

(Read Psalm 31:15a.) The Bible says our time is in God's hands. God has given us everything we see, everything we can touch, hear, feel or smell. He has given us time.

When we are planning our days, we need to remember that our time is a gift from God. We want to make him happy in the way we use our time. God can help us use our time wisely, if we will pray and ask him for help.

Prayer: God, thank you for the gift of time. Please help us to make time for the important parts of life - serving you and loving others. Amen.

50. Working For God...Labor Day...Galatians 6:9-10

We are celebrating a holiday tomorrow (or soon) called Labor Day. Why do we celebrate Labor Day? (Allow for responses.) On Labor Day we honor the workers in our country by giving many of them the day off from work to rest. Also, Labor Day can be a time to thank God for the jobs we have. We are thankful because jobs give us money to buy what we need. Jobs also give us a good feeling inside when we do well at them.

What kind of jobs do you have? (Some responses could be school work, chores around the house, helping Dad or Mom at work.)

How are jobs for adults different from jobs for kids? (Give the children time to answer.)

Some jobs are the same for adults and kids. Some are different. There is a job the Bible tells us all Christians have, no matter if they are kids or adults. (Read Galatians 6:9-10.) The job we all have is "doing good" to others. What does that mean? How can we do good to others? (Allow for responses.)

On Labor Day many people take the day off and don't do their jobs. Be we shouldn't take the day off from doing good. Raise your hand and tell me one way of doing good to others. Give time for each child to respond. Let's remember to always work at doing good to others, even on Labor Day.

Prayer: Jesus, thank you for jobs. Thank you that we all have jobs to do. Please help us to remember the jobs of doing good to others. Help us to do that job all year long. Amen.

51. Thankful Alphabet...Thanksgiving...Psalm 100:4-5

(As the children gather for this time together, have them sit in a circle.)

Raise your hand if you can tell me the holiday coming soon or the holiday we just celebrated. Thanksgiving. Why do we celebrate Thanksgiving? (Allow the children to respond.) On Thanksgiving we remember the Pilgrims, some of the first people to come to this country from England. They searched for a new home where they could be free to worship God. The Pilgrims celebrated Thanksgiving to thank God for the food they had grown and harvested through the summer and fall. Today when we celebrate Thanksgiving we thank God for the blessings he has given us.

Do you ever say "thank you" to God for the good things he gives us? Today we're going to thank God in a different way. We're going to use the alphabet to help us in our prayer of thanks.

(Select one child to begin. That child will choose something for which they are thankful that begins with the letter "A". Then they will say, "Thank you God, for..." and say the "A" blessing they have chosen. Continue around the circle with "B", "C" and so on. If you have a small group of children you can continue the alphabet blessings with the adults in the congregation to finish the alphabet. If you have a large group you can repeat some letters to include every child who wants to participate.)

After your group has completed the alphabet, say, "That was great! Thank you for sharing your thankfulness with me. God loves it when we say "thank you" to him." Then read Psalm 100:4-5.

Prayer: God, thank you for all these blessings and all these people in our church. Please help us to be thankful every day, not just at Thanksgiving. Amen.

52. More And More Christmas...Christmas...
Matthew 6:19-21

By now I'm sure all of you have noticed all the toy commercials on television. You might have opened your mailbox and found toy catalogs. How many of you have started planning your wish list for Christmas? (Allow for responses.)

Let's think way back to last Christmas. Do you remember what toys you received last year? Do you like to get presents? Why? (Give children time to share their answers.)

Presents can make us happy. Getting new toys is fun and it makes us feel good. But usually the fun doesn't last. After a while we get bored. Or something new comes along and we forget about the old. So we keep piling up more and more stuff as we get tired of what we have and we want some new.

Now having stuff isn't always bad. But when our having new things becomes all we can think about, then it's time to take another look at all of the things in our lives. Jesus said when we spend all our time thinking about our toys we don't have time to think about God. We think about what we have and what we don't have. Often we are jealous of the people we think have more things or nicer toys than we do.

When our thoughts are filled with what we have, we don't think about doing the things that make God happy. Our things become more important than making God happy. We can't think about God and what we have at the same time.

What would you do if Jesus asked you to sell your favorite toys and give the money to people who don't have money for food or clothes? Could you do it? (Give time for the children to respond.) Giving up our favorite things is very hard, but obeying Jesus should be the most important part of our lives.

Remember when you make out your Christmas list that toys aren't bad as long as Jesus is the center of our lives - not our things.

Prayer: Jesus, thank you for Christmas. Thank you for the love we show when we give each other gifts. Thank you for the money we have to buy gifts. Please help us to remember to put you at the center of our lives. Amen.

About the Authors

Heather Nall Hagler

Ken and Heather were married for over 21 years before her death from cancer in June 2016. Heather was a graduate of Asbury University, and Asbury Theological Seminary. She loved serving alongside her family at various churches in north Georgia. She worked as Director of Children and Family Ministries at Crossroads United Methodist Church and Buford First United Church in Buford, Georgia.

Heather was also a published curriculum writer with various Children's Ministry suppliers. In addition, she worked as a preschool teacher and teacher's assistant in many church preschools, including Hope Church in Dallas, GA and Cumming First United Methodist Preschool. She also enjoyed hiking and camping with her family and classic movies.

Ken Lee Hagler

Ken is a pastor and author of the book, "Life Sucks. Seek God," and has been in ministry full-time for over 20 years as a youth pastor, pastor and spiritual director. Ken regularly writes and produces videos under his unofficial title of "Jedi Pastor Ken" and you can find those links at www.kenhagler.com. Ken is a graduate of Asbury Theological Seminary and completed post-graduate studies at Garrett-Evangelical Theological Seminary. Ken is also a graduate of the The Upper Room's Two-Year Academy for Spiritual Formation.

Are You Ready To Write and Publish Your Book?

Yep, it can be done! I found the guidance and support I needed with Self-Publishing School and its creator and best-selling author, Chandler Bolt. From beginning to end, you'll find help and a supportive community of folks willing and able to share and encourage you along the way.

https://self-publishingschool.com

One Last Thing…

Thank you so much for purchasing and reading No Prep No Prop Children's Sermons. Heather meant this book to be a help to anyone and everyone wanting to share the Good News of Jesus Christ with Children. If you found this book to be meaningful and helpful for ministry, please leave a review on Amazon so other people can discover these simple but profound messages!

Made in the USA
Monee, IL
02 July 2020

35621022R00057